No Backbone!
The World of Invertebrates

Bloodthirsty Mosquitoes

by Meish Goldish

Consultant: Brian V. Brown
Curator, Entomology Section
Natural History Museum of Los Angeles County

BEARPORT
PUBLISHING

NEW YORK, NEW YORK

Credits

Cover, © Bryan Reynolds/Science Faction/Getty Images; 4–5, © Dwight Kuhn/Dwight Kuhn Photography; 6, © Johner Images/Getty Images; 7, © Pennsylvania Department of Conservation and Natural Resources-Forestry Archive, Bugwood.org; 9, © Bryan Reynolds/Science Faction/Getty Images; 11, © Ulrike Hammerich/Shutterstock; 13, © Dwight Kuhn/Dwight Kuhn Photography; 15, © Dwight Kuhn/Dwight Kuhn Photography; 17, © CDC/Jim Gathany, Inc.; 18, © Bartomeu Borrell/Superstock; 19, © Bartomeu Borrell/Superstock; 21, © CDC/Jim Gathany; 22TL, © Mark Cassino/SuperStock; 22TR, © Dwight Kuhn/Dwight Kuhn Photography; 22BL, © Stephen Dalton/Minden Pictures; 22BR, © Joseph Berger/Bugwood.org; 22Spot, © Little Miss Clever Trousers/Shutterstock; 23TL, © Jim Wehtje/Photodisc Green/Getty Images; 23TR, © Johner Images/Getty Images; 23BR, © Dwight Kuhn/Dwight Kuhn Photography.

Publisher: Kenn Goin
Editorial Director: Adam Siegel
Creative Director: Spencer Brinker
Design: Dawn Beard Creative
Photo Researcher: Elaine Soares

Library of Congress Cataloging-in-Publication Data

Goldish, Meish.
 Bloodthirsty mosquitoes / by Meish Goldish ; consultant, Brian V. Brown.
     p. cm. — (No backbone! The world of invertebrates)
 Includes bibliographical references and index.
 ISBN-13: 978-1-59716-585-3 (lib. bdg.)
 ISBN-10: 1-59716-585-9 (lib. bdg.)
 1. Mosquitoes—Juvenile literature. I. Brown, Brian Victor. II. Title.

 QL536.M35 2008
 595.77'2—dc22
                              2007032670

For more information, write to Bearport Publishing Company, Inc., 101 Fifth Avenue, Suite 6R, New York, New York 10003. Printed in the United States of America.

10 9 8 7 6 5 4 3 2 1

Contents

Little Flies

Mosquitoes are tiny **insects**.

They belong to the same group of insects as flies.

Like all flies, mosquitoes have two wings, two antennas, and six legs.

They also have a hard covering called an exoskeleton on the outside of their bodies.

The exoskeleton protects the soft parts of a mosquito's body.

The word *mosquito* comes from Spanish. It means "little fly."

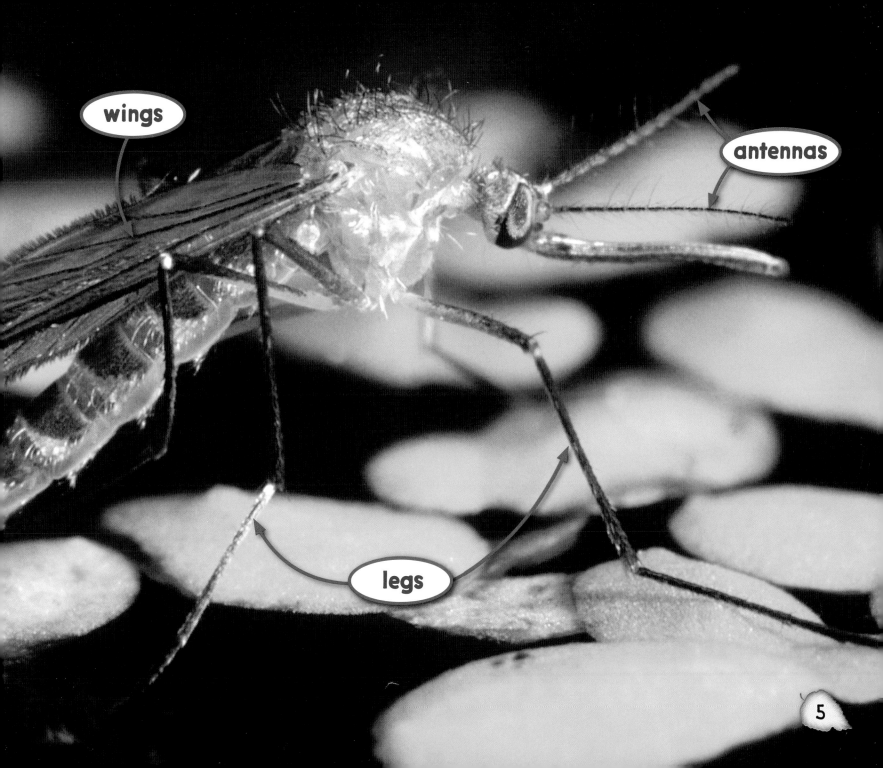

wings

antennas

legs

5

Thirsty for Food

Both male and female mosquitoes have a long, thin **beak** on their heads.

They use the beak to suck a sweet liquid called nectar from flowers.

Females also use it to poke a hole in the skin of animals and suck their blood.

They need the blood to make eggs inside their bodies.

beak

Some people call mosquitoes the vampires of the insect world.

Out for Blood

Female mosquitoes find their victims in many ways.

They use their two eyes to see creatures that are moving.

They use their two antennas to smell an animal's breath or sweat.

They also use them to feel the heat coming from the bodies of animals that are nearby.

There are about 3,000 kinds of mosquitoes. They bite animals such as cows, deer, and birds more often than they bite people.

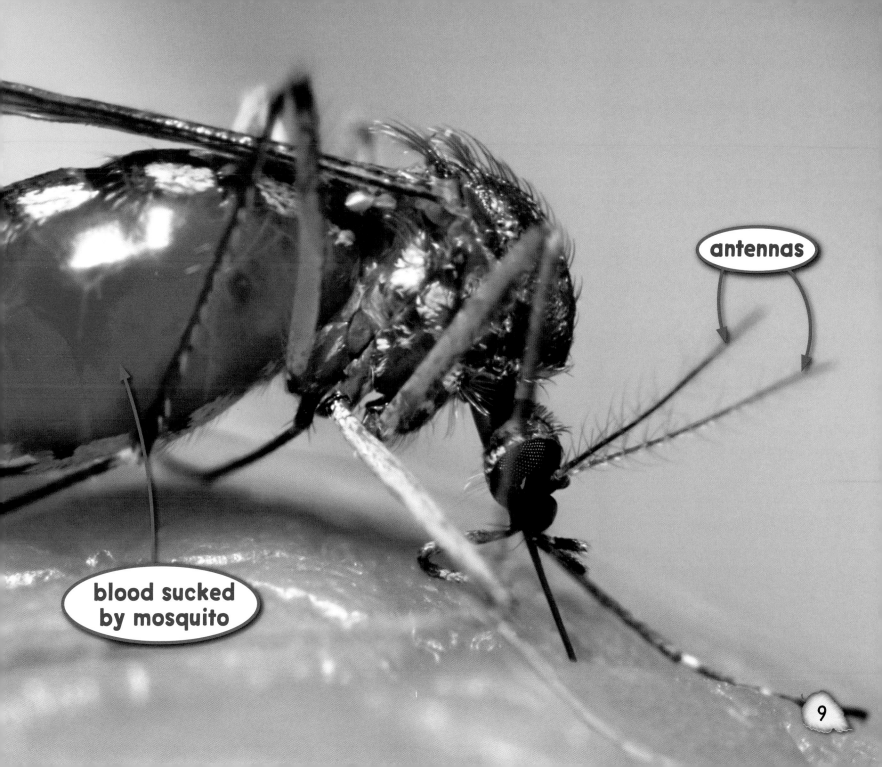

antennas

blood sucked
by mosquito

Carrying Disease

Mosquitoes are small, but they can be deadly.

Some kinds pass on diseases when they suck blood.

They can spread yellow fever and malaria.

Most mosquitoes don't make people sick, however.

They just leave an itchy red mark on a person's skin.

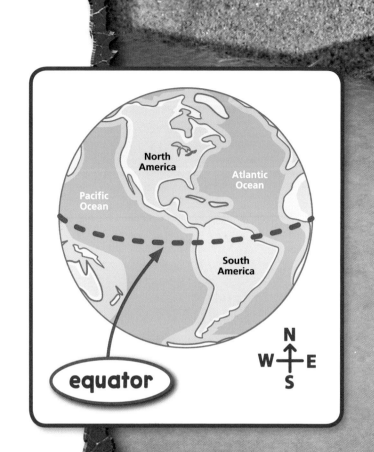

North America

Atlantic Ocean

Pacific Ocean

South America

N
W E
S

equator

Diseases carried by mosquitoes kill more than a million people each year. The danger from disease is greatest in hot countries near the **equator**.

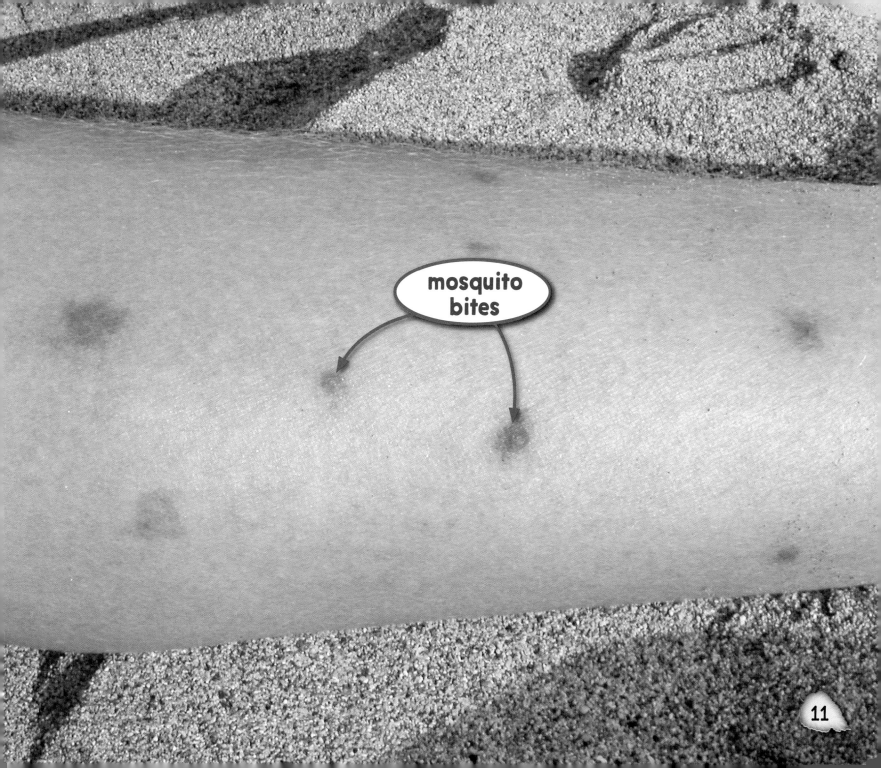

Mosquitoes on the Menu

Many different animals eat mosquitoes.

They include birds, bats, frogs, lizards, and spiders.

Dragonflies and other insects make meals of mosquitoes, too.

One kind of dragonfly can catch and eat up to 100 mosquitoes at a time.

Spiders often catch mosquitoes by trapping them in their sticky webs.

Eggs in Water

Most female mosquitoes lay their eggs in water.

The water might be in a pond or a puddle.

Sometimes it is in a tin can, a flowerpot, or a bucket.

The eggs float on the water.

They hatch in just a few days.

Some mosquitoes lay hundreds of eggs and stick them together. The group of floating eggs is called a raft.

mosquito eggs

Growing and Molting

After hatching in the water, a baby mosquito is a tiny worm-like creature called a larva.

A larva has an exoskeleton, but this covering cannot grow.

When the larva gets too big, its exoskeleton splits and comes off.

A new exoskeleton has been growing underneath.

The growing and shedding of an exoskeleton is called molting.

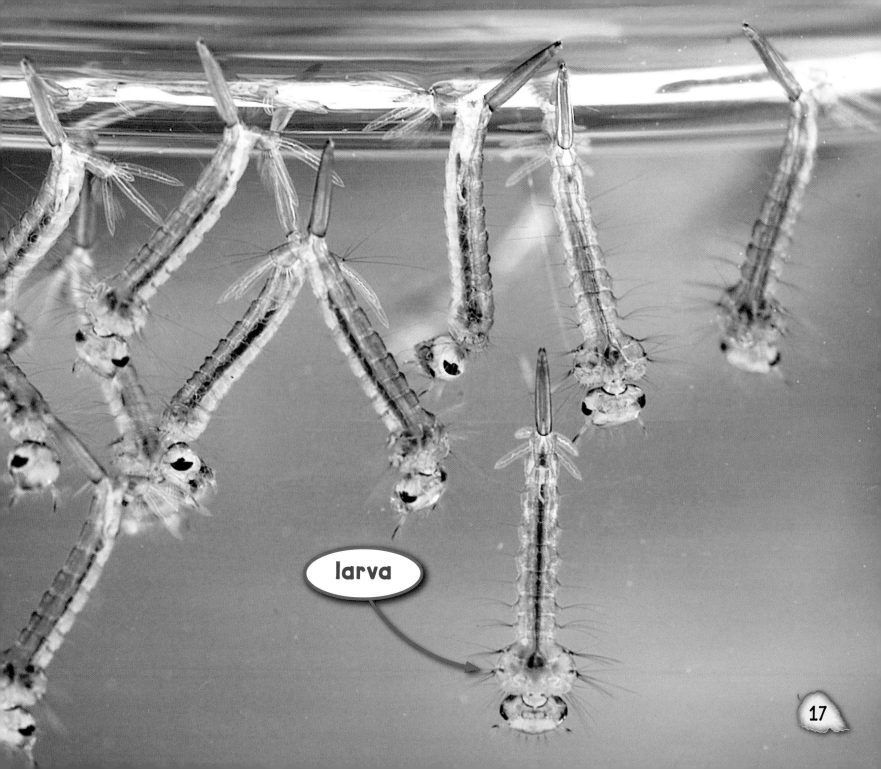

larva

Becoming an Adult

After its final molt, a larva changes shape.

Now it is called a pupa.

Its body is shaped like a comma, and it is covered by a hard case.

After a few days, the case splits open, and an adult mosquito comes out.

pupa

Frogs, fish, and dragonflies often eat eggs and baby mosquitoes that are floating in the water.

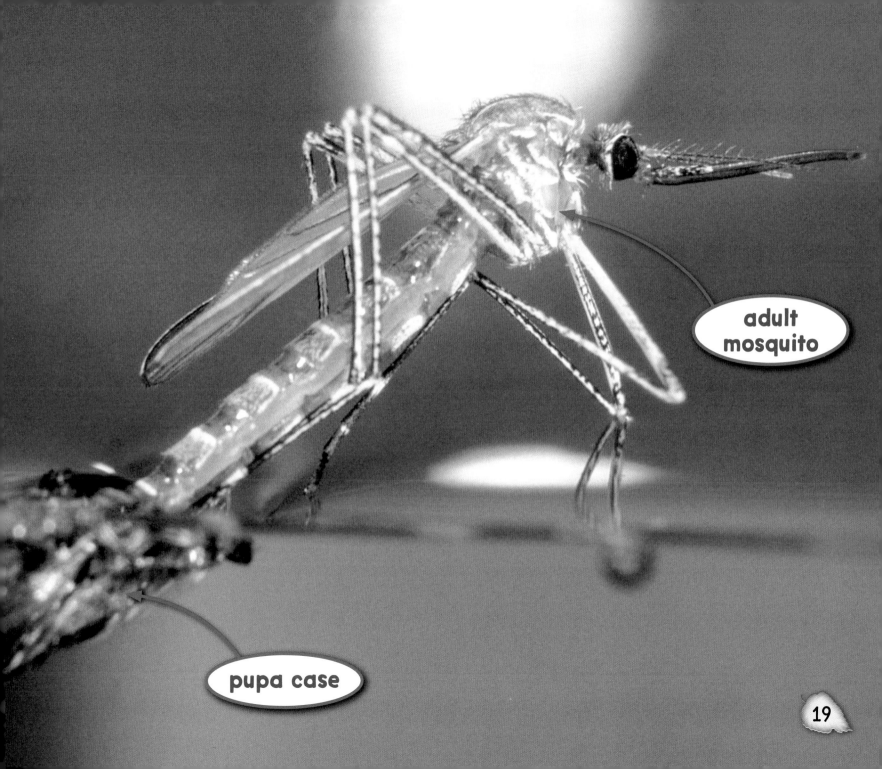

adult
mosquito

pupa case

19

A Short Life

Adult mosquitoes don't live very long.

Most live only a few weeks.

However, they leave behind plenty of young to carry on!

Mosquitoes can live almost anywhere on Earth, as long as they are near water so that they can lay their eggs.

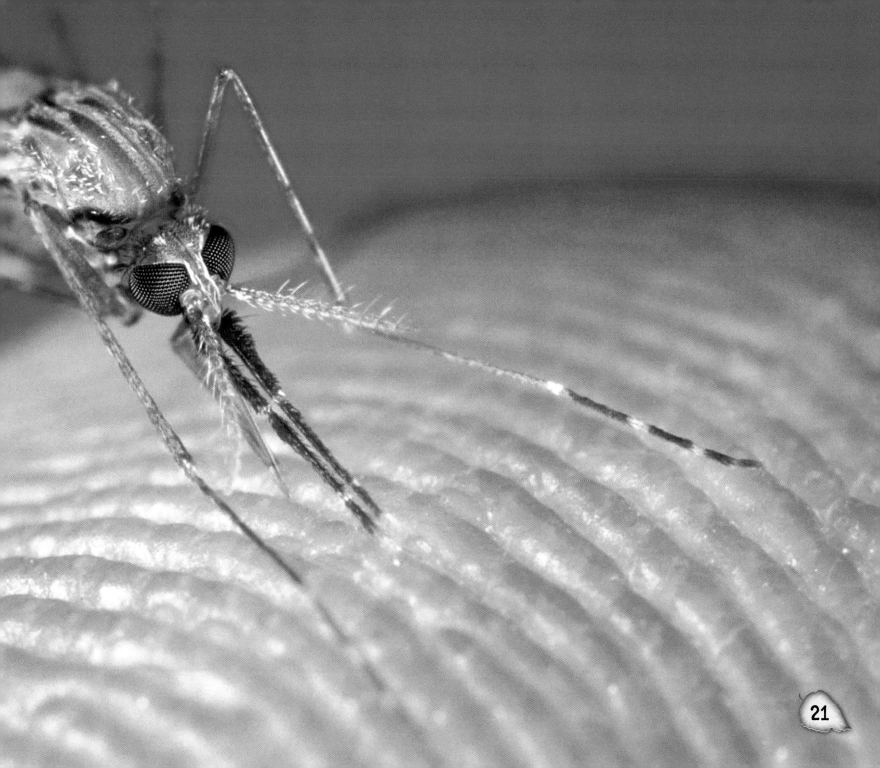

A World of Invertebrates

An animal that has a skeleton with a **backbone** inside its body is a *vertebrate* (VUR-tuh-brit). Mammals, birds, fish, reptiles, and amphibians are all vertebrates.

An animal that does not have a skeleton with a backbone inside its body is an *invertebrate* (in-VUR-tuh-brit). More than 95 percent of all kinds of animals on Earth are invertebrates.

Some invertebrates, such as insects and spiders, have hard skeletons—called exoskeletons—outside their bodies. Other invertebrates, such as worms and jellyfish, have soft, squishy bodies with no exoskeletons to protect them.

Here are four insects that are closely related to mosquitoes. Like all insects, they are invertebrates.

House Fly

Horse Fly

Fruit Fly

Gnat

Glossary

backbone
(BAK-*bohn*)
a group of
connected bones
that run along
the backs of some
animals, such as
dogs, cats, and fish;
also called a spine

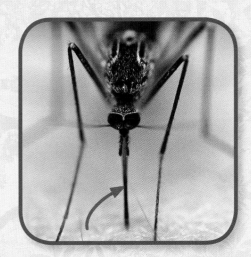

beak (BEEK)
the long, thin part
of a mosquito's
mouth used to
suck nectar from
flowers or blood
from animals

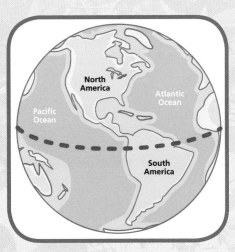

equator
(i-KWAY-tur)
an imaginary
line that runs
around the
middle of Earth

insects (IN-sekts)
small animals that
have six legs, three
main body parts,
two antennas, and
a hard covering
called an exoskeleton

Index

Read More

Bailey, Jill. *Mosquito*. Chicago: Heinemann (1998).

Kalman, Bobbie. *The Life Cycle of a Mosquito*. New York: Crabtree Publishing (2004).

Learn More Online

To learn more about mosquitoes, visit

www.bearportpublishing.com/NoBackbone-Insects

About the Author

Meish Goldish has written more than 100 books for children.
He lives in Brooklyn, New York.